■SCHOLASTIC

W9-DIW-959

Writing Lessons to Meet the Common Core

Grade 5

Linda Ward Beech

NEW YORK ● TORONTO ● LONDON ● AUCKLAND ● SYDNEY
MEXICO CITY ● NEW DELHI ● HONG KONG ● BUENOS AIRES

Teaching Resources

Edited by Mela Ottaiano
Cover design by Scott Davis
Interior design by Kathy Massaro
Image credits: page 15 © iStockphoto.com/studiocasper; page 36 © Marco Tomasini/Big Stock Photo;
page 39 © Lim Seng Kui/Big Stock Photo. All images © 2013.
Illustrations by Teresa Anderko, Hector Borlasca, Maxie Chambliss, Aleksey and Olga Ivanov, Margeaux Lucas

ISBN: 978-0-545-39164-1

Contents

About This Book

To build a foundation for college and career readiness, students need to learn to use writing as a way of offering and supporting opinions, demonstrating understanding of the subjects they are studying, and conveying real and imagined experiences and events. They learn to appreciate that a key purpose of writing is to communicate clearly to an external, sometimes unfamiliar audience, and they begin to adapt the form and content of their writing to accomplish a particular task and purpose.

—COMMON CORE STATE STANDARDS FOR ENGLISH LANGUAGE ARTS, JUNE 2010

This book includes step-by-step instructions for teaching the three forms of writing—Opinion, Informative/Explanatory, and Narrative—covered in the Common Core State Standards (CCSS). The CCSS are a result of a state-led effort to establish a single set of clear educational standards aimed at providing students nationwide with a high-quality education. The standards outline the knowledge and skills that students should achieve during their years in school.

The writing standards are a subset of the Common Core English Language Arts Standards. They provide "a focus for instruction" to help students gain a mastery of a range of skills and applications necessary for writing clear prose. This book is divided into three main sections; each section includes six lessons devoted to one of the writing forms covered in the CCSS for grade 5. You'll find more about each of these types of writing on pages 6–7.

- **Lessons 1–6** (pages 8–25) focus on the standards for writing opinion pieces.
- **Lessons 7–12** (pages 26–43) emphasize standards particular to informative/explanatory writing. (Lesson 7 focuses on the important skill of summarizing and paraphrasing information in research notes.)
- **Lessons 13–18** (pages 44–61) address the standards for narrative writing.

Although the CCSS do not specify how to teach any form of writing, the lessons in this book follow the gradual release of responsibility model of instruction: I Do It, We Do It, You Do It (Pearson & Gallagher, 1983). This model provides educators with a framework for releasing responsibility to students in a gradual manner. It recognizes that we learn best when a concept is demonstrated to us; when we have sufficient time to practice it with support; and when we are then given the opportunity to try it on our own. Each phase is equally important, but the chief goal is to teach for independence—the You Do It phase—so that students really learn to take over the skill and apply it in new situations.

Pearson, P. D., & Gallagher, M. C. (1983). "The Instruction of Reading Comprehension." *Contemporary Educational Psychology*, 8 (3).

A Look at the Lessons

The lessons in each section progress in difficulty and increase in the number of objectives and standards covered. This format enables you to use beginning or later lessons in a section depending on your students' abilities. Each lesson begins with a list of the objectives and standards. A general reproducible assessment checklist of standards for each writing form appears at the end of the book. (See pages 62–64.)

Here's a look at the features in each lesson.

Lesson Page 1

The first page is the teaching page of each lesson. It provides a step-by-step plan for using the student reproducible on the second lesson page and the On Your Own activity on the third lesson page. The teaching page closely follows the organization of the student reproducibles. This page also models sample text that students might generate when completing page 2 of the lesson. Finally, the teaching page includes an opportunity for students to review their classmates' work using the reproducible assessment checklist customized to the lesson's writing form. Each checklist also reminds students to check for correct spelling, punctuation, and paragraph form.

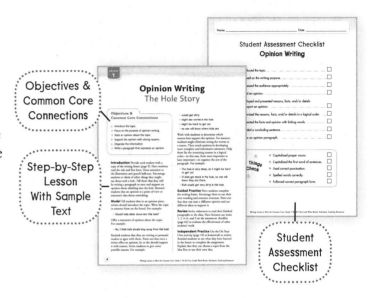

Objectives & Common Core Connections

Step-by-Step Lesson With Sample Text

Student Assessment Checklist

Lesson Page 2

The second page is a student reproducible, which is the core of the lesson. Students complete this writing frame as you guide them. In most lessons, students use the completed page as the basis for a paragraph they write on a separate sheet of paper.

Although you provide a model for completing this reproducible, you'll want to encourage students to use their own ideas, words, and sentences as much as possible.

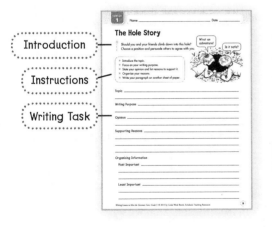

Introduction

Instructions

Writing Task

Lesson Page 3

The third page is a writing frame for independent work. It follows a format similar to the one students used for the first reproducible. Students choose their topic from the suggested list or use their own idea. In most lessons, students use the completed page as the basis for a paragraph they write on a separate sheet of paper.

Introduction

Topic Suggestions

Writing Task

Writing Lessons to Meet the Common Core: Grade 5 © 2013 by Linda Ward Beech, Scholastic Teaching Resources

Three Forms of Writing

The CCSS focus on three forms of writing— opinion, informative/explanatory, and narrative.

Opinion Pieces (Standards W.5.1, W.5.1a, W.5.1b, W.5.1c, W.5.1d)

The purpose of writing opinion pieces is to convince others to think or act in a certain way, to encourage readers or listeners to share the writer's point of view, beliefs, or position. Opinion pieces are also known as persuasive writing.

I think kids should stay away from this hole.

In developing an opinion piece, students must learn to introduce the topic, present a point of view, and supply valid reasons, facts, and expert opinions to support it. Phrases such as *I think, I believe, you should/should not* all signal persuasive writing.

I think a plant sale would be an excellent choice.

When teaching these lessons, display different examples of opinion pieces. You might include:

- editorials
- book, movie, TV, and theater reviews
- print advertisements
- letters to the editor
- letters of appeal
- feature columns

As students learn to produce different forms of writing, they are also enhancing their ability to recognize these forms in their reading.

Informative/Explanatory Writing (Standards W.5.2, W.5.2a, W.5.2b, W.5.2c, W.5.2d, W.5.2e)

The purpose of informative/explanatory writing is to inform the reader by giving facts, explanations, and other information. Informative/explanatory writing is also called expository writing.

When writing an informative/explanatory piece, students must introduce the topic and give facts, details, descriptions, and other information about the topic. The information should also be organized in a logical way. Many kinds of informative/explanatory writing require research. Sometimes illustrations are included with informative/explanatory pieces.

Antimacassars have a long history of being useful.

Display different examples of informative/ explanatory writing. You might include:

- reports
- news articles
- how-to articles
- biographies
- directions
- textbooks
- magazines
- recipes

Immediately bite off any overhanging pieces of ice cream.

Writing Lessons to Meet the Common Core: Grade 5 © 2013 by Linda Ward Beech, Scholastic Teaching Resources

Narrative Writing (Standards W.5.3, W.5.3a, W.5.3b, W.5.3c, W.5.3d, W.5.3e)

The purpose of narrative writing is to entertain. A narrative gives an account or a story. Usually, a narrative tells about something that happens over a period of time. Narratives can be true or imaginary.

"I know it's here!" exclaimed June.

When working on a narrative, students must develop a real or imagined experience or event. They must also establish a situation, or plot and setting, create characters, and recount events in a chronological sequence. Students use dialogue to show the feelings of characters and how they respond to events. Narratives often include sensory details.

One warm, sunny day, Bounce left home and got on a city bus.

When introducing narrative writing, display different examples. You might include:

- stories
- mysteries
- fables
- folktales
- myths
- science fiction
- friendly letters

Additional Writing Standards

Although this book focuses on the forms of writing called for in the CCSS, you can also incorporate the standards that relate to the production and distribution of writing and research to build and present knowledge. These standards include:

- W.5.4 Produce clear and coherent writing in which the development and organization are appropriate to task, purpose, and audience.

- W.5.5 Develop and strengthen writing as needed by planning, revising, editing, rewriting, or trying a new approach.

- W.5.6 Use technology to produce and publish writing as well as to interact with others; use keyboarding skills.

- W.5.7 Conduct short research projects that use several sources to build knowledge through investigation of different aspects of a topic.

- W.5.8 Recall relevant information from experiences or gather relevant information from print and digital sources; summarize or paraphrase information in notes and finished work, and provide a list of sources.

- W.5.9 Draw evidence from informational texts to support analysis, reflection, and research.

- W.5.10 Write routinely over extended and shorter time frames allowing for research, reflection, and revision.

Language Standards

You can also incorporate the CCSS Language Standards that focus on the conventions of standard English grammar and usage when writing or speaking (L.5.1); the conventions of standard English capitalization, punctuation, and spelling when writing (L.5.2); and the knowledge of language and its conventions when writing, speaking, reading, or listening (L.5.3).

Opinion Writing
The Hole Story

Introduction Provide each student with a copy of the writing frame (page 9). Have students read the title and first lines. Draw attention to the illustration and speech balloons. Encourage students to think of other things they might say about such a hole. Tell them that they will be writing a paragraph to state and support an opinion about climbing into the hole. Remind students that an opinion is a point of view or someone's idea about something.

Model Tell students that in an opinion piece, writers should introduce the topic. Write the topic in sentence form on the board. For example:

* Should kids climb down into this hole?

Offer a statement of opinion about the topic. For example:

* No, I think kids should stay away from this hole!

Remind students that they are writing to persuade readers to agree with them. Point out that once a writer offers an opinion, he or she should support it with reasons. Invite students to give some possible reasons. For example:

* would get dirty
* might see worms in the hole
* might be hard to get out
* no one will know where kids are

Work with students to determine which reasons best support the opinion. For instance, students might eliminate seeing the worms as a reason. Then coach students in developing more complete and informative sentences. Help them list the remaining reasons in a logical order—in this case, from most important to least important—to organize the rest of the paragraph. For example:

* The hole is very deep, so it might be hard to get out.
* If kids get stuck in the hole, no one will know they are there.
* Kids would get very dirty in this hole.

Guided Practice Have students complete the writing frame. Encourage them to use their own wording and sentence structure. Point out that they can state a different opinion and use different ideas to support it.

Review Invite volunteers to read their finished paragraphs to the class. Have listeners use items 1, 2, 4–6, and 9 on the assessment checklist (page 62) to evaluate the effectiveness of other students' work.

Independent Practice Use the On Your Own activity (page 10) as homework or review. Remind students to use what they have learned in the lesson to complete the assignment. Explain that they can choose a topic from the Idea Box or use their own idea.

The Hole Story

Should you and your friends climb down into this hole?
Choose a position and persuade others to agree with you.

- Introduce the topic.
- Focus on your writing purpose.
- State your opinion and list reasons to support it.
- Organize your reasons.
- Write your paragraph on another sheet of paper.

Topic _____

_____

Writing Purpose _____

_____

Opinion _____

_____

Supporting Reasons _____

_____

_____

_____

Organizing Information

Most Important _____

_____

_____

Least Important _____

_____

_____

Name _____ Date _____

On Your Own

Choose a daring activity from the Idea Box or think of one of your own. Form an opinion about the safety of the activity. Complete this page. Then, write a paragraph on another sheet of paper to persuade others to agree with you.

Idea Box

○ Walking on Top of a Fence

○ Riding a Bike While Pulling Someone on Skates Behind You

○ Hanging Upside Down From a High Tree Branch

○ My Idea: _____

_____

_____

_____

Topic _____

_____

Writing Purpose _____

_____

Opinion _____

_____

Supporting Reasons _____

_____

_____

_____

Organizing Information

Most Important _____

_____

_____

Least Important _____

_____

_____

Writing Lessons to Meet the Common Core: Grade 5 © 2013 by Linda Ward Beech, Scholastic Teaching Resources

Opinion Writing
Fund-Raising Fun

Objectives &
Common Core Connections

* Introduce the topic.
* Focus on the purpose of opinion writing.
* State an opinion about the topic.
* Support the opinion with strong reasons.
* Organize the information.
* Write a paragraph that expresses an opinion.

Introduction Provide each student with a copy of the writing frame (page 12). Have students read the title and first lines. Draw attention to the illustrations and captions. Tell students that they will be writing a paragraph to state and support an opinion about what the class could do to raise money.

Model Tell students that in an opinion piece, writers should introduce the topic. Write the topic in sentence form on the board. For example:

* The class can hold a bake sale or a plant sale to raise money.

Remind students that an opinion is a point of view or someone's idea about something. Offer an opinion in sentence form about the topic. For example:

* I think a plant sale would be an excellent choice.

Say: *The purpose of opinion writing is to persuade someone to agree with your opinion and think or act in a certain way. I have stated an opinion, and now I want to support it with reasons.* For example:

* plants very popular with buyers
* help us learn about plants

* good for the environment
* grow plants we sell
* plants need care
* brighten a room
* make science lessons more interesting

Work with students to determine which reasons best support the opinion. Help students recognize that "plants need care" does not support the opinion. Guide students in organizing the remaining reasons in a logical way. For instance, the reasons related to buyers might be grouped together and the reasons concerning students might be grouped together. Work with students to develop complete sentences. For example:

* Plants brighten up a room and are very popular with buyers. They are also good for the environment.

* A plant sale will make science lessons more interesting. It will help students learn more about plants. We can grow the plants we sell.

Guided Practice Have students complete the writing frame. They may state a different opinion and use different ideas to support it. Encourage students to use their own wording and sentence structure. Point out that they can choose either the plant sale or the bake sale as their topic.

Review Invite volunteers to read their finished paragraphs to the class. Have listeners use items 1, 2, 4–6, and 9 on the assessment checklist (page 62) to evaluate the effectiveness of other students' work.

Independent Practice Use the On Your Own activity (page 13) as homework or review. Remind students to use what they have learned to complete the assignment. Explain that they can choose a topic from the Idea Box or use their own idea.

Name _____ Date _____

Fund-Raising Fun

 Suppose your class wants to raise money. Should you have a plant sale or a bake sale? Take a position and persuade others to agree with you.

 Good for the Environment

- Introduce the topic.
- Focus on your writing purpose.
- State your opinion and list reasons to support it.
- Organize your reasons.
- Write your paragraph on another sheet of paper.

 Good to Eat

Topic _____

_____

Writing Purpose _____

_____

Opinion _____

_____

Supporting Reasons _____

_____

_____

_____

Organizing Information

Group 1 _____

_____

_____

Group 2 _____

_____

_____

Writing Lessons to Meet the Common Core: Grade 5 © 2013 by Linda Ward Beech, Scholastic Teaching Resources

On Your Own

Choose a way your school can raise money from the Idea Box or think of one of your own. Complete this page. Then, write a paragraph on another sheet of paper to persuade others to agree with you.

Idea Box

○ Car Wash   ○ My Idea:

○ Book Fair   _____

○ Walkathon   _____

Topic _____

_____

Writing Purpose _____

_____

Opinion _____

_____

Supporting Reasons _____

_____

_____

_____

Organizing Information

Group 1 _____

_____

_____

Group 2 _____

_____

_____

Opinion Writing
Plenty of Plastic

Objectives & Common Core Connections

* Introduce the topic for a selected audience.
* Focus on the purpose of opinion writing.
* State an opinion about the topic.
* Develop a list of facts to support the opinion.
* Organize the information.
* Write a paragraph that expresses an opinion.

Introduction Provide each student with a copy of the writing frame (page 15). Have students read the title and first lines. Point out the picture of the plastic shopping bag and the captions. Tell students that they will write a paragraph for an imaginary school newspaper in which they state and support their opinions with facts. Remind them that a fact is information that can be proved, so writers must often research facts. Have some relevant reference materials ready.

Model Offer a sentence to introduce the topic. For example:

* Should people use plastic shopping bags?

Remind students that writers should keep their audience in mind. Have students identify that the readers of a school newspaper might be primarily students. Talk about how a writer might engage this audience by using a friendly, conversational approach to state an opinion. For example:

* You probably carry things in a plastic shopping bag several times a week. However, you can be a better friend to the environment if you stop using these plastic bags.

Suggest some more facts or have students research facts to support this opinion. For example:

* made from petroleum, a nonrenewable resource
* clog drains
* litter landscape
* cause flooding

Work with students to determine the best order—in this case, from most important to least important—in which to organize the facts. Model how to create sentences from the facts. For example:

* Plastic bags are made from petroleum, an oil-based product. Oil is a nonrenewable resource. Many used plastic bags end up littering the landscape because they do not decay quickly. Plastic bags also clog roadside drains and cause flooding.

Guided Practice Have students complete the writing frame. Encourage them to use their own wording and sentence structure. Point out that they can state a different opinion and use different facts to support it. Direct students to do research to find additional facts to support their opinions.

Review Invite volunteers to read their finished paragraphs to the class. Have listeners use items 1–6 and 9 on the assessment checklist (page 62) to evaluate the effectiveness of other students' work.

Independent Practice Use the On Your Own activity (page 16) as homework or review. Explain that students can choose a topic from the Idea Box or use their own idea. Remind students to use what they have learned in the lesson to complete the assignment. Point out that they will need to do research to find facts for their topic. Have appropriate reference materials and a computer with Internet access available for student research.

Writing Lessons to Meet the Common Core: Grade 5 © 2013 by Linda Ward Beech, Scholastic Teaching Resources

Name _____ Date _____

Plenty of Plastic

⭐ What is your opinion about using plastic bags?
Write a paragraph for a school newspaper
to persuade readers to agree with you.

It's great for
carrying things.

It doesn't
decompose.

It can be
dangerous
for children
to play with.

- Introduce the topic with your audience in mind.
  Remember to focus on your writing purpose.
- State your opinion and give facts to support it.
- Organize the facts.
- Write your paragraph on another sheet of paper.

It keeps things dry.

Topic _____

_____

Audience _____

Opinion _____

_____

Supporting Facts _____

_____

_____

_____

_____

Organizing Information

Most Important _____

_____

_____

Least Important _____

_____

_____

Name _____ Date _____

On Your Own

Choose a common product from the Idea Box or think of one of your own. Form an opinion about using the product you have chosen. Complete this page. Then, write a paragraph on another sheet of paper to persuade others to agree with you.

Idea Box

○ Foam Egg Carton   ○ My Idea:

○ Aerosol Can

_____

○ Roll of Paper Towels

_____

Topic _____

_____

Audience _____

Opinion _____

_____

Supporting Facts _____

_____

_____

_____

Organizing Information

Most Important _____

_____

_____

Least Important _____

_____

Opinion Writing
People of the Past

**Objectives &
Common Core Connections**

* Introduce the topic for a selected audience.
* Focus on the purpose of opinion writing.
* State an opinion about the topic.
* Develop a list of facts and details to support the opinion.
* Organize the information.
* Write a paragraph that expresses an opinion.

Introduction Provide each student with a copy of the writing frame (page 18). Have students read the title and first lines. Draw attention to the illustrations of the knight and the Viking. Tell students that they will be writing a paragraph to persuade the class which topic to study.

Model Say: *First, I must introduce the topic.* Write the topic in sentence form on the board. For example:

* We can study either knights or Vikings in our social studies class.

Remind students that writers should keep their audience—in this case, classmates—in mind. Offer an opinion in sentence form. For example:

* Knights would be an amazing topic because they were so unique. Here are just a few details that we'd learn.

Point out that including details—additional pieces of information—to facts helps a reader understand something better. Suggest facts and details about knights. For example:

* wore armor including helmet and gauntlets
* had coat of arms or badge on shield
* honor to be a knight

* lived code of conduct called chivalry
* carried sword and lance
* loyal to their lord

Guide students in organizing the information. Some facts and details tell about a knight's equipment. Others tell about what it meant to be a knight. Model how to create sentences from the information. For example:

* Each knight had his own badge, called a coat of arms, on his shield. He wore a suit of armor with a special helmet in battle. Even his gloves, known as gauntlets, were metal! A knight fought with either his sword or lance.
* It was an honor to be a knight. A knight lived by a code of conduct called chivalry and was always loyal to his lord.

Guided Practice Have students complete the writing frame. Point out that they can choose either the knights or Vikings as their topic. Encourage students to use their own wording and sentence structure. Remind them to use other facts and details that they know or have researched. Provide some relevant materials.

Review Invite volunteers to read their finished paragraphs to the class. Have listeners use items 1–6 and 9 on the assessment checklist (page 62) to evaluate the effectiveness of other students' work.

Independent Practice Use the On Your Own activity (page 19) as homework or review. Explain that students can choose a topic from the Idea Box or use their own idea. Remind students to use what they have learned in the lesson to complete the assignment. Point out that they will need to do research to find facts and details for their topic. Have appropriate reference materials and a computer with Internet access available for student research.

Name _____ Date _____

People of the Past

You and your classmates have to choose
a social studies project. Should it be about
knights or Vikings? Take a position and
persuade others to agree with you.

- Introduce the topic with your audience in mind.
  Remember to focus on your writing purpose.
- State your opinion and give facts and details to support it.
- Organize the information.
- Write your paragraph on another sheet of paper.

Topic _____

Audience _____

Opinion _____

_____

Supporting Facts and Details _____

_____

_____

_____

_____

Organizing Information

Group 1 _____

_____

_____

_____

Group 2 _____

_____

_____

Writing Lessons to Meet the Common Core: Grade 5 © 2013 by Linda Ward Beech, Scholastic Teaching Resources

Name _____ Date _____

On Your Own

Choose a topic for a class social studies project from the Idea Box or think of one of your own. Complete this page. Then, write a paragraph on another sheet of paper to persuade others to agree with you.

Idea Box

○ Pioneers   ○ My Idea:

○ Ancient Greeks   _____

○ Ancient Egyptians _____

Topic _____

Audience _____

Opinion _____

_____

Supporting Facts and Details _____

_____

_____

_____

_____

Organizing Information

Group 1 _____

_____

_____

_____

Group 2 _____

_____

Opinion Writing
Add a Sport

Objectives & Common Core Connections

✳ Introduce the topic for a selected audience.

✳ Focus on the purpose of opinion writing.

✳ State an opinion about the topic.

✳ Develop a list of facts to support the opinion.

✳ Organize the information.

✳ Use linking words to connect the reasons and opinion.

✳ Write a paragraph that expresses an opinion.

Introduction Provide each student with a copy of the writing frame (page 21). Have students read the title and first lines. Point out the illustration. Tell students that they will be writing a paragraph to persuade officials to start a volleyball team for your school.

Model Say: *I need to introduce the topic for my audience—school officials who are thinking about the cost of such a program and the benefits to students.* For example:

- A volleyball team would be a great addition to our school sports program.

List facts to support this opinion. For example:

- can be played indoors or outdoors
- only equipment is a net and a ball
- team sport
- programs in almost all states
- game of strategy

Coach students in developing complete and more informative sentences to use in a paragraph. Model how the opinion and some facts might be connected with linking words and phrases, such as *consequently, because,* or *for instance.* Guide students in organizing the information. In this case, some sentences relate to the cost factor, while others address benefits to students. For example:

- This sport can be played on either an indoor or an outdoor court. The only equipment needed is a net and a ball. Consequently, volleyball is not as expensive as other sports. Most states have official volleyball programs so resources for coaching and scheduling are available.

- Volleyball promotes good sportsmanship because it is a team sport in which players depend on one another. Students also learn strategy, a useful life skill.

Guided Practice Have students complete the writing frame. Encourage them to use their own wording and sentence structure. Students may wish to do research to find additional facts to support their opinion.

Review Invite volunteers to read their finished paragraphs to the class. Have listeners use items 1–7 and 9 on the assessment checklist (page 62) to evaluate the effectiveness of other students' work.

Independent Practice Use the On Your Own activity (page 22) as homework or review. Remind students to use what they have learned in the lesson to complete the assignment. Explain that they can choose a topic from the Idea Box or use their own idea.

Name _____ Date _____

Add a Sport

Suppose your school plans to start a new sports team. You think it should be a volleyball team. Write a paragraph to school officials to persuade them to agree with you.

- Introduce the topic with your audience in mind. Remember to focus on your writing purpose.
- State your opinion and give facts to support it.
- Organize the information.
- Use linking words to connect your opinion with the facts.
- Write your paragraph on another sheet of paper.

Topic _____

Audience _____

Opinion _____

_____

Supporting Facts _____

_____

_____

_____

_____

Possible Linking Words _____

Organizing Information

Group 1 _____

_____

_____

Group 2 _____

_____

Name _____ Date _____

On Your Own

Choose a sport for a community team from the Idea Box or think of one of your own. Complete this page. Then, write a paragraph on another sheet of paper to persuade others to agree with you.

Idea Box

○ Lacrosse   ○ My Idea:

○ Soccer   _____

○ Baseball   _____

Topic _____

Audience _____

Opinion _____

_____

Supporting Facts _____

_____

_____

_____

_____

Possible Linking Words _____

Organizing Information

Group 1 _____

_____

_____

Group 2 _____

_____

Opinion Writing
A Call for Carrots

Objectives & Common Core Connections

* Introduce the topic for a selected audience.
* Focus on the purpose of opinion writing.
* State an opinion about the topic.
* Develop a list of facts to support the opinion.
* Organize the information.
* Use linking words to connect the reasons and opinion.
* Write a concluding sentence.
* Write a paragraph that expresses an opinion.

Introduction Provide each student with a copy of the writing frame (page 24). Have students read the title and first lines. Draw attention to the illustration. Tell students that they will be writing a paragraph to persuade state leaders to make the carrot the official state vegetable.

Model Say: *I must introduce the topic for my audience—state officials who may have other vegetables in mind.* For example:

* I believe the carrot would be the perfect state vegetable.

Invite students to suggest facts to support this opinion. For example:

* has Vitamin A, good for eyes
* healthy snack
* can eat raw or cooked
* can be stored for several months
* inexpensive
* lots of minerals

Coach students in developing complete and more informative sentences to use in a paragraph.

Model how the opinion and some facts might be connected with linking words and phrases, such as *consequently*, *since*, or *for instance*. Guide students in organizing the information. In this case, some sentences relate to health and nutrition, while others relate to convenience. For example:

* This orange root vegetable provides many health benefits such as Vitamin A, which is important for eyesight. The carrot also has a lot of the minerals that the body needs. Consequently, the carrot is a healthy snack. It can be eaten raw or cooked in many different ways. The carrot is inexpensive and can be stored in a cool place for several months.

Explain that a persuasive paragraph usually has a concluding sentence that restates the writer's opinion. For example:

* Since the carrot is so versatile, it would be a popular state vegetable.

Guided Practice Have students complete the writing frame. Encourage them to use their own wording and sentence structure.

Review Invite volunteers to read their finished paragraphs to the class. Have listeners use items 1–9 on the assessment checklist (page 62) to evaluate the effectiveness of other students' work.

Independent Practice Use the On Your Own activity (page 25) as homework or review. Explain that students can choose a topic from the Idea Box or use their own idea. Remind students to use what they have learned in the lesson to complete the assignment. Point out they will need to do research for their topic. Have appropriate reference materials and a computer with Internet access available for student research.

Name _____ Date _____

A Call for Carrots

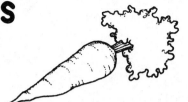

You want the carrot to be your state vegetable. Write
a paragraph to persuade state officials to agree with you.

- Introduce the topic with your audience in mind. Remember to focus
  on your writing purpose.
- State your opinion, give facts to support it, and organize your information.
- Use linking words to connect your opinion with the facts.
- Provide a concluding sentence.
- Write your paragraph on another sheet of paper.

Topic _____

Audience _____

Opinion _____

_____

Supporting Facts _____

_____

_____

_____

Possible Linking Words _____

Organizing Information

   Group 1 _____

_____

_____

   Group 2 _____

_____

Concluding Sentence _____

_____

Name _____ Date _____

On Your Own

Choose an item for a school symbol from the Idea Box or think of one of your own. Complete this page. Then, write a paragraph on another sheet of paper to persuade others to agree with you.

Idea Box

○ Tree   ○ Flower   ○ Animal

○ My Idea: _____

Topic _____

Audience _____

Opinion _____

_____

Supporting Facts _____

_____

_____

_____

Possible Linking Words _____

Organizing Information

　Group 1 _____

_____

_____

　Group 2 _____

_____

Concluding Sentence _____

_____

Informative Writing
Moving Around

Objectives & Common Core Connections

* Introduce the topic.
* Focus on the purpose of informative writing.
* Conduct research to find facts and examples.
* Summarize or paraphrase information in notes.

Introduction Provide each student with a copy of the writing frame (page 27). Have students read the title and first lines. Tell them that they will develop facts for a paragraph about animal migration. Point out that the purpose of informative writing is to inform readers. Explain that it is usually necessary to do research for this kind of writing. Have appropriate reference materials and a computer with Internet access available for student research.

Model You might say: *The topic is animal migration.* Point out that although the sample text on page 27 gives some information about this topic, writers can't simply copy it. Stress that when students do research, they must take notes and paraphrase the information by putting it in their own words. Suggest that they look for key words such as *animals, migration, season, scarce,* and *abundant* before taking notes. For example:

* migration—animals move from place to place on regular basis
* use same route, move in same season
* move in cold season when food is scarce
* move to where food plentiful

Coach students in developing sentences from their notes. For example:

* Some animals migrate by moving from place to place on a regular basis. They use the same route and move in the same season each time. Animals migrate to find food, which becomes scarce in cold seasons.

Direct students to use the research materials you have assembled to find examples of animals that migrate on land, sea, and water. Have them record notes. For example:

* land—bison
* sea—whales, seals, salmon
* air—terns, bats, Monarch butterflies

Guided Practice Have students complete the writing frame. Encourage them to use their own wording and sentence structure.

Review Invite volunteers to read their notes and sentences to the class. Have listeners use items 1, 2, 4, and 5 on the assessment checklist (page 63) to evaluate the effectiveness of other students' work.

Independent Practice Use the On Your Own activity (page 28) as homework or review. Remind students to use what they have learned in the lesson to complete the assignment. Explain that they can choose a topic from the Idea Box or use their own idea. Have appropriate reference materials and a computer with Internet access available for student research.

Writing Lessons to Meet the Common Core: Grade 5 © 2013 by Linda Ward Beech, Scholastic Teaching Resources

Name _____ Date _____

Moving Around

Many animals migrate.
What does this mean?
Why do they do it?

- Name the topic.
- Focus on your writing purpose.
- Look for key words.
- Take notes in your own words.
- Write practice sentences from your notes.
- Do your own research to find examples of animals that migrate by land, sea, and air.

Topic _____

Writing Purpose _____

Sample Text:

The regular movement of some animals from one place to another along the same route in the same season is known as migration. Migration enables many species to leave places where food becomes scarce during cold seasons and move to places where food is more abundant.

Key Words _____

_____

Practice Notes _____

_____

_____

Practice Sentences _____

_____

_____

_____

Research and Notes _____

_____

_____

Practice Sentences _____

_____

_____

Name _____ Date _____

On Your Own

Choose a topic from the Idea Box or think of one of your own. Complete this page.

Idea Box

○ Hibernation   ○ Camouflage   ○ Herbivores

○ My Idea: _____

Topic _____

Writing Purpose _____

Key Words _____

Research and Notes _____

_____

_____

_____

_____

_____

_____

_____

Practice Sentences _____

_____

_____

_____

_____

_____

Informative Writing
Landforms

Objectives & Common Core Connections

* Introduce the topic.
* Focus on the purpose of informative writing.
* Develop the topic with researched facts, word definitions, and an illustration.
* Organize the information to make the topic clear.
* Write an informative paragraph.

Introduction Provide each student with a copy of the writing frame (page 30). Have students read the title and first line and study the illustration. Tell them that they will write an informative paragraph to describe what a peninsula is. Point out that the purpose of this kind of writing is to provide information. Remind students that it is usually necessary to do research for informative writing and have some relevant materials ready.

Model Suggest a sentence to introduce and define the topic. For example:

* A peninsula is an area of land surrounded by water on three sides but still connected to the mainland.

Explain that the next step is to develop an informative paragraph using researched facts and examples about the topic. For example:

* found all over Earth
* example—Florida
* from Latin words meaning "almost island"
* Michigan—two peninsulas
* example—Italy
* often small areas of land

Coach students in organizing the information to make it easier for a reader to understand. In this case, some facts tell more about a peninsula in general, while others give examples of peninsulas. Help students form complete sentences from the information. For example:

* In fact, the word peninsula comes from Latin words meaning "almost island." Peninsulas are found all over Earth. Many are small, but some are very large. The state of Florida is a peninsula. Another state, Michigan, is made up of two peninsulas. In Europe, the country of Italy is a peninsula.

Discuss how the illustration on page 30 helps a reader understand what a peninsula is.

Guided Practice Have students complete the writing frame. Encourage them to use their own wording and sentence structure and to draw their own illustration on a separate sheet of paper.

Review Invite volunteers to read their finished paragraphs to the class. Have listeners use items 1, 2, 5, 6, 10, 13, and 15 on the assessment checklist (page 63) to evaluate the effectiveness of other students' work.

Independent Practice Use the On Your Own activity (page 31) as homework or review. Tell students they can choose a landform from the Idea Box or use their own idea. Remind students to use what they learned in the lesson to complete the assignment. Point out that they will need to do research for their topic. Have appropriate reference materials and a computer with Internet access available for student research. Provide additional paper so students can draw an illustration to go with their paragraphs.

Landforms

What is a peninsula?

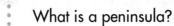

GULF OF
MEXICO

Florida

ATLANTIC
OCEAN

- Introduce the topic.
- Focus on your writing purpose.
- Research and list facts and examples about the topic.
- Define key words.
- Organize the information to make the topic clear.
- Write your paragraph on another sheet of paper to explain what a peninsula is.
- Add an illustration to help your readers.

Topic _____

Writing Purpose _____

Facts _____

_____

_____

_____

Examples _____

_____

Definitions _____

_____

Organizing Information

Group 1 _____

_____

_____

Group 2 _____

_____

Name _____ Date _____

On Your Own

Choose a landform from the Idea Box or think of one of your own. Complete this page. Then, write a paragraph on another sheet of paper to explain what the landform is. Include an illustration.

Idea Box

○ Isthmus   ○ Strait   ○ Canyon

○ My Idea: _____

Topic _____

Writing Purpose _____

Facts _____

_____

_____

_____

Examples _____

_____

Definitions _____

_____

Organizing Information

Group 1 _____

_____

_____

Group 2 _____

_____

_____

Explanatory Writing
How to Eat an Ice Cream Cone

Objectives & Common Core Connections

* Introduce the topic for a selected audience.
* Focus on the purpose of explanatory writing.
* List the steps and develop them with detailed information.
* Organize the steps in a logical order.
* Include a quotation.
* Write an explanatory paragraph.

Introduction Provide each student with a copy of the writing frame (page 33). Have students read the title and first line and study the illustration. Point out that an explanatory paragraph can tell how to do something. Tell students that they will write a paragraph explaining how to eat an ice cream cone without dripping. The paragraph will be posted as a sign in an ice cream shop so their audience will be ice cream customers.

Model Say: *The audience for this paragraph— ice cream shop customers—might respond to a little humor.* Suggest a sentence to introduce the topic. For example:

* Eating an ice cream cone without dripping is a challenge, but you can do it!

List steps that will help readers. For example:

* nibble at cone's edge
* immediately bite off any overhanging pieces
* lick around perimeter while turning cone
* be sure scoop is in cone securely
* continue licking
* push ice cream down

Coach students in organizing the information in a logical way. Help students develop complete sentences from the information. Point out that including details will make it more useful. For example:

* Begin by making sure the ice cream is securely in the cone. Immediately bite off any overhanging pieces of ice cream. Then lick upward in a spiral around the ice cream while turning the cone. After each lick, push the ice cream down gently with your tongue. Repeat until the ice cream is level with the cone. Nibble at the cone edge until the cone and ice cream are gone.

Tell students that sometimes a quotation adds to an explanation. In this case, it adds some humor. For example:

* "If it's a hot day, eat quickly!" says Bob, our customer of the week.

Guided Practice Have students complete the writing frame. Encourage them to use their own wording and sentence structure. Some students may enjoy adding humorous illustrations.

Review Invite volunteers to read their finished paragraphs to the class. Have listeners use items 1–3, 7, 10–12, and 15 on the assessment checklist (page 63) to evaluate the effectiveness of other students' work.

Independent Practice Use the On Your Own activity (page 34) as homework or review. Remind students to use what they have learned in the lesson to complete the assignment. Tell students they can choose a messy food from the Idea Box or use their own idea.

Name _____ Date _____

How to Eat an Ice Cream Cone

⭐ Explain how to eat an ice cream cone *without dripping.*

- Introduce the topic with your audience in mind.
- Focus on your writing purpose.
- List the steps and include details.
- Organize the steps in logical order.
- Include a quotation.
- Write a paragraph on another sheet of paper to explain how to eat an ice cream cone.

Topic _____

Audience _____

Writing Purpose _____

Steps With Details _____

_____

_____

_____

_____

Organizing Information

First _____

_____

_____

_____

_____

Last _____

Quotation _____

_____

Writing Lessons to Meet the Common Core: Grade 5 © 2013 by Linda Ward Beech, Scholastic Teaching Resources

Name _____ Date _____

On Your Own

From the Idea Box, choose a food that is challenging to eat without getting messy or think of your own idea. Complete this page. Then, write a paragraph on another sheet of paper to explain how to eat the food.

Idea Box

- ○ Barbecued Ribs
- ○ Lobster
- ○ Burrito

- ○ My Idea:

_____

_____

Topic _____

Audience _____

Writing Purpose _____

Steps With Details _____

_____

_____

_____

_____

_____

Organizing Information

First _____

_____

_____

_____

_____

Last _____

Quotation _____

_____

Informative Writing
The Wombat

**Objectives &
Common Core Connections**

* Introduce the topic for a selected audience.
* Focus on the purpose of informative writing.
* Develop the topic with researched facts and examples.
* Use domain-specific words and precise language.
* Organize the information to make the topic clear.
* Write an informative paragraph.

Introduction Provide each student with a copy of the writing frame (page 36). Review the page and tell students that they will be writing a paragraph for a science book explaining what a wombat is. Remind students that it is necessary to do research for informative writing and have some relevant materials ready.

Model Suggest a sentence to introduce the topic for readers of a science book. For example:

* A wombat is a short, furry animal that lives in Australia.

Explain that the next step is to develop information using facts you have researched. For example:

* marsupial—kind of mammal
* digs and lives in burrows
* herbivore with rodent-like front teeth
* carries young in backward pouch
* aggressive when attacked
* weighs up to 75 pounds

Point out that because you are writing for a science book, you are using words such as *marsupial* and *mammal* that are specific to animal science. You are also using precise or exact language, such as *rodent-like front teeth*.

Coach students in organizing the information in a logical way. In this case, some facts give the characteristics of wombats, while others describe their behavior. Guide students in developing complete sentences from the information. For example:

* The wombat is a marsupial, a kind of mammal that carries its young in a pouch. Unlike other marsupials, a wombat's pouch opens facing the back. A wombat can weigh up to 75 pounds. It is an herbivore with rodent-like front teeth to gnaw tough vegetation such as bark, roots, and grasses. The wombat uses its teeth and sharp claws to dig the burrows in which it lives. When attacked, a wombat can be very aggressive.

Guided Practice Have students complete the writing frame. Encourage them to use their own wording and sentence structure.

Review Invite volunteers to read their finished paragraphs to the class. Have listeners use items 1–3, 5, 8, 10, and 15 on the assessment checklist (page 63) to evaluate the effectiveness of other students' work.

Independent Practice Use the On Your Own activity (page 37) as homework or review. Tell students they can choose an animal from the Idea Box or use their own idea. Remind students to use what they learned in the lesson to complete the assignment. Point out that they will need to do research for their topic. Have appropriate reference materials and a computer with Internet access available for student research. Provide additional paper and invite students to include an illustration to go with their paragraph.

The Wombat

What is a wombat?

- Introduce the topic with your audience in mind. Remember to focus on your writing purpose.
- Research and list facts and examples about the topic.
- Use science words and precise language.
- Organize the information to make the topic clear.
- Write your paragraph on another sheet of paper to explain what a wombat is.

Topic _____

Audience _____

Facts and Examples _____

_____

_____

_____

_____

_____

Science/Precise Words _____

_____

Organizing Information

   Group 1 _____

_____

_____

_____

   Group 2 _____

_____

Name _____ Date _____

On Your Own

Choose an animal from the Idea Box or think of one of your own. Complete this page. Then, write a paragraph on another sheet of paper to explain what the animal is.

Idea Box

○ Tapir   ○ Sloth   ○ Mandrill

○ My Idea: _____

Topic _____

Audience _____

Facts and Examples _____

_____

_____

_____

_____

Science/Precise Words _____

_____

Organizing Information

Group 1 _____

_____

_____

Group 2 _____

_____

Informative Writing
The Big Durian

Objectives & Common Core Connections

* Introduce the topic for a selected audience.
* Focus on the purpose of informative writing.
* Develop the topic with researched facts, examples, and word definitions.
* Organize the information to make the topic clear.
* Use linking words to connect ideas.
* Write an informative paragraph.

Introduction Provide each student with a copy of the writing frame (page 39). Review the page and tell students that they will be writing a paragraph for grocery store owners explaining what a durian is. Remind students that it is usually necessary to do research for informative writing and have some relevant materials ready.

Model Suggest a sentence to introduce and define the topic—durians—for grocery store owners. For example:

* The durian is a unique fruit from Southeast Asia.

Explain that the next step is to develop information using the information you have researched. Note that it is helpful to define unfamiliar words such as *husk* and *odor*. For example:

* overpowering odor or smell
* thorn-covered outer covering called husk
* both flesh and seeds edible
* large in size and weight
* popular in many traditional dishes
* very flavorful

Coach students in organizing the information in a logical way. In this case, some facts describe the durian, while others tell how it is used. Guide students in developing complete sentences from the information. Model how the information might be connected with linking words, such as *also, because,* or *especially*. For example:

* A durian has an outer covering called a husk that is covered with sharp thorns. It is <u>also</u> a large fruit, often 12 inches long, six inches wide, and weighing seven pounds. Although the durian has an overpowering odor, or smell, its soft inside, called the flesh, has a flavorful taste. <u>Because</u> it is so tasty, the durian is a popular ingredient in Southeast Asian cooking. Both the flesh and the seeds are used in many traditional dishes.

Guided Practice Have students complete the writing frame. Encourage them to use their own wording and sentence structure. Students may wish to do additional research to find other facts for their explanations.

Review Invite volunteers to read their finished paragraphs to the class. Have listeners use items 1–3, 5, 6, 9, 10, and 15 on the assessment checklist (page 63) to evaluate the effectiveness of other students' work.

Independent Practice Use the On Your Own activity (page 40) as homework or review. Tell students they can choose a food from the Idea Box or use their own idea. Remind them to use what they learned in the lesson to complete the assignment. Point out that they will need to do research for their topic. Have appropriate reference materials and a computer with Internet access available for student research. Provide additional paper and invite students to include an illustration to go with their paragraph.

The Big Durian

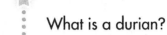

What is a durian?

- Introduce the topic with your audience in mind. Remember to focus on your writing purpose.
- Research and list facts and examples about the topic.
- Define key words.
- Use linking words to connect ideas.
- Organize the information to make the topic clear.
- Write a paragraph on another sheet of paper to explain what a durian is.

Topic _____

Audience _____

Facts and Examples _____

_____

_____

_____

_____

Definitions _____

Possible Linking Words _____

_____

Organizing Information

Group 1 _____

_____

_____

Group 2 _____

_____

_____

Name _____ Date _____

On Your Own

Choose an unusual food from the Idea Box or think of one of your own. Complete this page. Then, write a paragraph on another sheet of paper to explain what the food is.

Idea Box

○ Lychee   ○ Kumquat   ○ Pomegranate

○ My Idea: _____

Topic _____

Audience _____

Facts and Examples _____

_____

_____

_____

_____

Definitions _____

Possible Linking Words _____

_____

Organizing Information

Group 1 _____

_____

_____

Group 2 _____

_____

_____

Informative Writing
Household Words

Objectives & Common Core Connections

* Introduce the topic for a selected audience.
* Focus on the purpose of informative writing.
* Develop the topic with researched facts, examples, and word definitions.
* Organize the information to make the topic clear.
* Use linking words to connect ideas.
* Write a concluding sentence.
* Write an informative paragraph.

Introduction Provide each student with a copy of the writing frame (page 42). Review the page and tell students that they will be writing a paragraph for users of a Web site to help people build their vocabulary. Remind students that it is usually necessary to do research for informative writing and have some relevant materials ready.

Model Suggest sentences to introduce the topic. For example:

> • You've probably used one, but didn't know what to call it. An *antimacassar* is a protective cloth or covering for furniture.

Guide students in developing information for the paragraph. For example:

* name from macassar hair oil
* decorative
* placed on arms of chairs
* found on planes, buses
* used on headrests of sofas
* prevent soiling

Coach students in organizing the information in a logical way. Point out that it can be loosely placed in two groups: information about why an antimacassar is used and about how it is used. Guide students in developing complete sentences from the information. Model how information might be connected with linking words, such as *also, because,* or *another*. For example:

> • The name for these cloths comes from the macassar oil that people used in their hair in the 1800s. <u>Because</u> this oil soiled furniture, antimacassars were made to protect the upholstery. *Anti* means "against." Housewives placed antimacassars on the arms and backs of chairs and sofas. Sometimes a set of antimacassars was <u>also</u> used for decorative purposes. Today, you might find antimacassars on the headrests of plane, train, or bus seats.

Explain that an informative paragraph usually has a concluding sentence. For example:

> • Antimacassars have a long, useful history.

Guided Practice Have students complete the writing frame. Encourage them to use their own wording and sentence structure as well as other information that they know or have researched about antimacassars.

Review Invite volunteers to read their finished paragraphs to the class. Have listeners use items 1–3, 5, 6, 9, 10, 14, and 15 on the assessment checklist (page 63) to evaluate the effectiveness of other students' work.

Independent Practice Use the On Your Own activity (page 43) as homework or review. Tell students they can choose a household word from the Idea Box or use their own idea. Remind students to use what they learned in the lesson to complete the assignment. Point out that they will need to do research for their topic. Have appropriate reference materials and a computer with Internet access available for student research.

Household Words What is an antimacassar?

- Introduce the topic with your audience in mind. Remember to focus on your writing purpose.
- Research and list facts and examples about the topic.
- Define key words.
- Use linking words to connect ideas.
- Organize the information to make the topic clear.
- Provide a concluding sentence.
- Write a paragraph on another sheet of paper.

Topic _____

Audience _____

Facts and Examples _____

_____

_____

_____

_____

_____

Definitions _____

_____

Possible Linking Words _____

Organizing Information

   Group 1 _____

_____

_____

   Group 2 _____

_____

Concluding Sentence _____

Name _____ Date _____

On Your Own

Choose a household item from the Idea Box or think of one of your own. Complete this page. Then, write a paragraph on another sheet of paper to explain what the item is.

Idea Box

○ Ottoman   ○ Sham   ○ Sconce

○ My Idea: _____

Topic _____

Audience _____

Facts and Examples _____

_____

_____

_____

_____

Definitions _____

_____

Possible Linking Words _____

Organizing Information

Group 1 _____

_____

_____

Group 2 _____

_____

Concluding Sentence _____

_____

Narrative Writing
Surprise Visitor

Objectives & Common Core Connections

* Focus on the purpose of narrative writing.
* Establish a situation.
* Establish characters.
* Write a good opening sentence.

Introduction Provide each student with a copy of the writing frame (page 45). Have students read the title and first line. Discuss the illustration. Ask students what story they think is suggested. Talk about whether the story is real or imagined. Explain to students that they will develop a narrative piece about the picture. Remind them that a narrative is a story or account of something and is usually written to entertain the reader.

Model Point out that a story needs a good beginning so that the reader will want to continue. Provide an opening sentence to summarize the situation (scene, plot, setting) suggested by the illustration. For example:

* All of a sudden the space alien from the TV show was in the room with Walker.

Mention that you have just given the boy in the illustration a name. Coach students in describing what else the illustration shows. For example:

* Walker has been watching TV
* math book on couch
* Walker looks surprised
* alien looks friendly

Guide students in developing the characters and situation. For example:

* Walker is in fifth grade. He's supposed to be doing his math homework, but instead has been watching his favorite TV show. Math is not his best subject, and he has a test tomorrow.
* The alien is named Lex. He plays the leading role on the TV show. He has seen the math book on the couch and knows that Walker will get in trouble if he doesn't study for his test.

Guided Practice Have students complete the writing frame. Encourage them to use their own ideas about the situation and characters. Guide students in developing the situation further by asking: *Now that he is in the living room, what will Lex do? Will he help Walker? What else might happen?* Suggest that students develop a narrative about the characters and situation on another sheet of paper. Some students may wish to illustrate their narrative.

Review Invite volunteers to share their finished pages with the class. Have listeners use items 1 and 3–5 on the assessment checklist (page 64) to evaluate the effectiveness of students' work.

Independent Practice Use the On Your Own activity (page 46) as homework or review. Remind students to use what they learned in the lesson to complete the assignment. Explain that students can choose a topic from the Idea Box or use one of their own. Provide paper so that students can illustrate their story ideas and characters.

Name _____ Date _____

Surprise Visitor

Use the picture to tell a story.

- Focus on your writing purpose.
- Tell what is happening.
- Tell who the characters are.
- Begin with a good opening sentence.

Writing Purpose _____

_____

What Is Happening _____

_____

_____

_____

_____

_____

Character 1 _____

_____

_____

Character 2 _____

_____

_____

Opening Sentence _____

_____

_____

On Your Own

Choose a story topic from the Idea Box or think of your own. Complete this page. Draw a picture to go with your story ideas on another sheet of paper.

Idea Box

○ Museum Statue Comes to Life   ○ My Idea: _____

○ Pet Dog Begins to Talk   _____

○ Hidden Tunnel Leads to Secret World   _____

Writing Purpose _____

_____

What Is Happening _____

_____

_____

_____

_____

_____

Character 1 _____

_____

_____

Character 2 _____

_____

_____

Opening Sentence _____

_____

_____

Narrative Writing
Sticky Situation

Objectives & Common Core Connections

✳ Focus on the purpose of narrative writing.

✳ Address the audience appropriately.

✳ Establish a situation and characters.

✳ Write a good opening sentence.

✳ Organize the events in a logical sequence.

✳ Use dialogue to show characters' responses.

✳ Write a narrative.

Introduction Provide each student with a copy of the writing frame (page 48). Discuss the title and illustrations. Tell students that they will use the illustrations to develop a narrative for fifth graders. Review that a narrative is a story or account of something and is usually written to entertain the reader.

Model Summarize the situation and discuss the characters. Say: *A girl can't find her science report, and both she and her teacher are upset. Finally, she finds it in the wrong folder.* Encourage students to think about each character in the situation. Model sentences to begin the narrative in a way that appeals to an audience of fifth graders. For example:

- June could not believe her science report wasn't in her folder. It had to be there— she had packed it herself!

Mention that you have named the girl in the illustrations. Coach students in describing what the pictures show. For example:

- June really upset
- searches through papers
- June confused; teacher not pleased
- science report in language arts folder

Explain that a writer can use dialogue to show how a character feels and responds to an event. For example:

- "I know it's here!" exclaimed June.
- "I can't give you credit if you don't turn it in," warned Miss Epson.

Remind students that a narrative has a beginning, middle, and end. Review the sequence of events in the pictures. Work with students to develop complete sentences and dialogue to narrate the story. For example:

- June looked and looked, but the report wasn't there. "I know it's here!" exclaimed June. She was terribly upset. "I must have lost it," she said sadly, thinking of all the times she'd said she lost homework, but really hadn't done it. This time she *had* done it. "I can't give you credit if you don't turn it in," warned Miss Epson. Later, when it was time for language arts, June got another surprise. There, in her language arts folder, was her science report! "Congratulations!" smiled Miss Epson.

Guided Practice Have students complete the writing frame. Encourage them to use their own ideas for dialogue. Be sure to review how to use capitalization and punctuation in dialogue.

Review Invite volunteers to share their finished narratives with the class. Have listeners use items 1–7 and 12 on the assessment checklist (page 64) to evaluate the effectiveness of students' work.

Independent Practice Use the On Your Own activity (page 49) as homework or review. Remind students to use what they learned in the lesson to complete the assignment. Explain that students can choose a topic from the Idea Box or use one of their own. Also suggest that they title their finished narratives.

Sticky Situation

⭐ Use the pictures to tell the story.

- Focus on your writing purpose and keep your audience in mind.
- Tell what is happening and who the characters are.
- Organize the events in a logical sequence.
- Use dialogue to show how the characters respond to events.
- Write your narrative on another sheet of paper.

Writing Purpose/Audience _____

What Is Happening _____

_____

_____

_____

Character 1 _____

Character 2 _____

Opening Sentence _____

Order of Events _____

_____

_____

_____

Dialogue _____

_____

_____

_____

Name _____ Date _____

On Your Own

Choose a topic from the Idea Box or think of your own topic. Complete this page. Then, write your narrative on another sheet of paper.

Idea Box

○ Girl Forgets to Give Father a Message

○ Boy Is Late for Team Practice

○ Man Leaves Borrowed Umbrella on Bus

○ My Idea: _____

_____

_____

Writing Purpose/Audience _____

What Is Happening _____

_____

_____

_____

Character 1 _____

Character 2 _____

Opening Sentence _____

Order of Events _____

_____

_____

_____

Dialogue _____

_____

_____

Narrative Writing
Fill the Shoes

Objectives & Common Core Connections

✳ Focus on the purpose of narrative writing.

✳ Address audience appropriately.

✳ Establish a situation/setting and characters.

✳ Write a good opening sentence.

✳ Organize the events in a logical sequence.

✳ Use dialogue to show characters' responses.

✳ Write a narrative.

Introduction Provide each student with a copy of the writing frame (page 51). Discuss the title and illustrations. Tell students that they will write a narrative for a youth magazine about two characters wearing this footwear.

Model Draw attention to the title and identify who might be wearing the two pairs of shoes. Say: *I think a carpenter is in the work boots and a ballerina is wearing the toe shoes. Now, why would these two people be in the same story?* Write down some ideas. For example:

- carpenter works in theater
- dancer is rehearsing
- dancer spins around a post
- post is loose
- carpenter dances onstage to save dancer
- carpenter should be in the act

Point out that the situation you have established sets the narrative in a theater. Explain that a setting is where a story takes place. Model sentences to begin the narrative. Remind students that you want it to appeal to young readers of a magazine. For example:

- Carl walked quietly through the backstage of the theater. He stopped briefly to watch a dancer rehearsing on stage.

Mention that you have given the carpenter a name. Then, explain that a writer can use dialogue to show how a character feels and responds to an event. For example:

- "Uh-oh!" said Carl as the dancer spun around a post that was part of the scenery. "That post is loose! If it falls, so does she."

Remind students that a narrative has a beginning, middle, and end. Explain that you have established the beginning and are now developing the middle part of the story. Work with students to develop complete sentences for the next events. For example:

- Suddenly, Carl, too, spun into action. Gracefully, he danced onto the stage and with a quick tap of his hammer made the post secure. As he danced away, the dancer called after him, "Thanks! Come back for the performance tonight. I could use a partner!"

Guided Practice Have students complete the writing frame. Encourage them to use their own ideas for dialogue.

Review Invite volunteers to share their finished narratives with the class. Have listeners use items 1–7 and 12 on the assessment checklist (page 64) to evaluate the effectiveness of students' work.

Independent Practice Use the On Your Own activity (page 52) as homework or review. Remind students to use what they have learned in the lesson to complete the assignment. Explain that they can choose a topic from the Idea Box or use one of their own.

Name _____ Date _____

Fill the Shoes

Who wears these shoes? What story can you tell?

- Focus on your writing purpose and keep your audience in mind.
- Tell what is happening, what the situation or setting is, and who the characters are.
- Organize the events in a logical sequence.
- Use dialogue to show how the characters respond to events.
- Write your narrative on another sheet of paper.

Writing Purpose/Audience _____

What Is Happening _____

_____

_____

_____

Setting _____

Character 1 _____

Character 2 _____

Opening Sentence _____

Order of Events _____

_____

_____

_____

Dialogue _____

_____

_____

_____

Name _____ Date _____

On Your Own

Choose two pairs of shoes from the Idea Box or think of two pairs of your own. Complete this page. Then, write your narrative on another sheet of paper about the people in the shoes.

Idea Box

○ Cowboy Boots and Flip Flops

○ High Heels and Running Shoes

○ Bedroom Slippers and Fur-lined Snow Boots

○ My Idea: _____

_____

_____

_____

Writing Purpose/Audience _____

What Is Happening _____

_____

_____

_____

Setting _____

Character 1 _____

Character 2 _____

Opening Sentence _____

Order of Events _____

_____

_____

_____

Dialogue _____

_____

_____

Writing Lessons to Meet the Common Core: Grade 5 © 2013 by Linda Ward Beech, Scholastic Teaching Resources

Narrative Writing
Do-Over

Objectives & Common Core Connections

✳ Focus on the purpose of narrative writing.

✳ Establish a situation and characters.

✳ Write a good opening sentence.

✳ Develop the narrative with description.

✳ Organize the events in a logical sequence.

✳ Write a first-person narrative.

Introduction Provide each student with a copy of the writing frame (page 54). Discuss the title and illustration. Tell students they will develop a first-person narrative about cooking a meal. Remind students that a first person narrative uses the pronoun *I*.

Model Summarize the situation in the illustration and discuss who the characters are and what their expressions show. Explain that the *I* in this narrative will be the boy who has cooked the meal. Model a sentence to begin the narrative. For example:

- I spent all afternoon making a macaroni dish for Mom and Kevin.

Point out that writers use description to help readers understand better. For example:

- There it was, piled high in a red dish with a creamy cheese sauce on top. I'd even added parsley for a colorful effect.

Coach students in using the illustration to develop ideas about what happens. For example:

- older boy serves macaroni
- Kevin takes a bite and makes a face

- mother looks puzzled
- boy forgot an ingredient
- boy is upset, and mother offers a "do-over"

Remind students that a narrative has a beginning, middle, and end. Explain that you have established the beginning and are now developing the middle part of the story. Work with students to develop complete sentences for the next events and to use description. For example:

- I served the dish and waited nervously. Kevin took a big helping and then a big bite. The expression on his face was awful. Then, Mom ate a spoonful. She looked puzzled. I tried a bite. It was awful, like glue that was hardening. Had I forgotten something? Suddenly, it came to me—I had added the cheese and flour, but forgotten the milk! It was such a blow; I cringed in shame. But Mom said she knew I was a good cook, and we should have a "do-over" next week. That made me feel better.

Guided Practice Have students complete the writing frame. Encourage them to use their own ideas for description.

Review Invite volunteers to share their finished narratives with the class. Have listeners use items 1, 3–6, 8, and 12 on the assessment checklist (page 64) to evaluate the effectiveness of students' work.

Independent Practice Use the On Your Own activity (page 55) as homework or review. Remind students to use what they learned in the lesson to complete the assignment. Explain that they can choose a topic from the Idea Box or use one of their own. Encourage students to title their finished narratives.

Do-Over

What happens when you make a mistake?

- Remember to focus on your writing purpose.
- Tell what is happening and who the characters are.
- Write a good opening sentence.
- Use description to help reader.
- Organize the events in a logical sequence.
- Write your first-person narrative on another sheet of paper.

What Is Happening _____

_____

_____

Character 1 _____

Character 2 _____

Character 3 _____

Opening Sentence _____

Description _____

_____

_____

_____

_____

Order of Events _____

_____

_____

_____

_____

Name _____ Date _____

On Your Own

Choose one of the mistakes from the Idea Box or think of your own. Complete this page. Then, write a first person narrative on another sheet of paper about the mistake and a "do-over."

Idea Box

○ Choosing Wrong Size for a Gift   ○ My Idea: _____

○ Misreading Directions on a Test   _____

○ Making a Mistake While Knitting   _____
    a Sweater   _____

What Is Happening _____

_____

_____

Character 1 _____

Character 2 _____

Character 3 _____

Opening Sentence _____

Description _____

_____

_____

_____

_____

Order of Events _____

_____

_____

_____

Narrative Writing
A Dog's Life

Objectives & Common Core Connections

❋ Establish a situation and characters.

❋ Write a good opening sentence.

❋ Organize the events in a logical sequence.

❋ Use sensory and transitional words.

❋ Write a narrative.

Introduction Provide each student with a copy of the writing frame (page 57). Discuss the title and illustration. Ask students what story they think is suggested. Tell students that they will develop a narrative about the dog in the picture.

Model Summarize the situation in the picture as you see it. Say: *A dog is riding on a bus by himself. I wonder where he's going. Where is his owner?* Model a sentence to begin a narrative. For example:

● Bounce thought of himself as a very good pet. However, April, his owner, was sometimes too busy to play with him. So Bounce decided to take a day off from being a pet.

Mention that you have named the characters. Coach students in using the illustration to list some ideas about what happens. For example:

● Bounce leaves home

● gets on a bus

● has good adventures

● returns home

● April welcomes him back

● Bounce promises himself more days off

Point out that a writer sometimes uses sensory words to give readers a better picture of things.

Explain that most sensory words are adjectives that tell more about the five senses. For example:

● One <u>warm</u>, <u>sunny</u> day, Bounce left home and got on a city bus.

Explain that you have developed the beginning of the narrative and are now working on the rest. Guide students in developing complete sentences for the next events. Point out that a writer often uses transitional words, such as *next*, *then*, and *after*, to manage the pacing of a sequence of events. For example:

● He got off at the first stop to visit the meat market. The smell of fresh hamburger led him right to the door. He knew the butcher would have some tasty scraps. <u>Next</u>, Bounce joined some children on a playground. <u>After</u> he had caught their ball numerous times, he took a bath by running through a fountain. <u>Then</u>, he settled on a bench for a nice nap. <u>Finally</u>, Bounce took a bus back home. April was happy to see him and promised to play with him every day. Even so, Bounce thought he would take days off now and then.

Guided Practice Have students complete the writing frame. Remind them to include sensory and transitional words.

Review Invite volunteers to share their finished narratives with the class. Have listeners use items 3–6, 9, 10, and 12 on the assessment checklist (page 64) to evaluate the effectiveness of students' work.

Independent Practice Use the On Your Own activity (page 58) as homework or review. Remind students to use what they have learned in the lesson to complete the assignment. Explain that they can choose a topic from the Idea Box or use one of their own. Encourage students to title their finished narratives.

Name _____ Date _____

A Dog's Life

What goes on in the mind of a pet?

- Tell what is happening and who the characters are.
- Organize the events in order.
- Use sensory words to help the reader.
- Use transitional words to manage the sequence.
- Write your narrative on another sheet of paper.

What Is Happening _____

_____

_____

_____

_____

Character 1 _____

_____

Character 2 _____

_____

Order of Events _____

_____

_____

_____

_____

Sensory Words _____

_____

Transitional Words _____

_____

Name _____ Date _____

On Your Own

Choose one of the pets from the Idea Box or think of one of your own. Complete this page. Then, write an imaginary narrative on another sheet of paper about that pet.

Idea Box

○ Cat   ○ Rabbit   ○ Parrot

○ My Idea: _____

What Is Happening _____

_____

_____

_____

_____

Character 1 _____

_____

Character 2 _____

_____

Order of Events _____

_____

_____

_____

_____

Sensory Words _____

_____

Transitional Words _____

_____

Writing Lessons to Meet the Common Core: Grade 5 © 2013 by Linda Ward Beech, Scholastic Teaching Resources

Narrative Writing
Early Spring

Objectives & Common Core Connections

❋ Establish a situation and characters.

❋ Write a good opening sentence.

❋ Organize the events and use transitional words.

❋ Use dialogue.

❋ Write a concluding sentence.

❋ Write a narrative.

Introduction Provide each student with a copy of the writing frame (page 60). Have students read the title and first line. Discuss the illustration. Ask students what story they think is suggested. Tell them that they will develop a narrative about the picture.

Model Summarize the situation as you see it. Say: *A park worker is staring at a trash can full of broken umbrellas. I wonder what she's thinking? What is she going to do?* Point out that a writer can use dialogue to show what a character is thinking. Model sentences to begin a narrative. For example:

> "What a miserable, rainy day," thought Lucia as she made her rounds in the park. It had been a long, dreary winter, and she missed seeing things in bloom. She stopped as she saw a trash bin overflowing with broken umbrellas. The wind had blown them inside-out.

Mention that you have given the woman in the illustration a name. Coach students in using the illustration as a springboard for ideas about what happens. For example:

> • upset at unsightly mess

> • gathers up umbrellas
> • goes home for weekend
> • returns to work on Monday
> • places umbrella flower sculpture in park

Explain that you have developed the beginning of the narrative and now must work on the middle and end. Guide students in developing complete sentences for the next events. For example:

> Lucia was upset at the unsightly mess. She gathered up the inside-out umbrellas before she went home for the weekend. When she returned to work on Monday, she had a large package. It was a sculpture of flowers made from umbrella spokes. Lucia placed it near the trash bin .

Point out that a narrative has an ending or conclusion. For example.

> "Now the park has flowers!" she said. "Spring is on its way."

Guided Practice Have students complete the writing frame. Remind students to include transitional words and dialogue.

Review Invite volunteers to share their finished narratives with the class. Have listeners use items 3–7, 10, 11, and 12 on the assessment checklist (page 64) to evaluate the effectiveness of students' work.

Independent Practice Use the On Your Own activity (page 61) as homework or review. Remind students to use what they have learned in the lesson to complete the assignment. Explain that they can choose a topic from the Idea Box or use one of their own. Also suggest that students title their finished narratives.

Early Spring

★ How can you make a mess beautiful?

- Tell what is happening and who the character is.
- Use dialogue to show the character's feelings.
- Organize the events with transitional words.
- Use a concluding sentence or two to end the story.
- Write your narrative on another sheet of paper.

What Is Happening _____

_____

_____

Character _____

_____

Dialogue _____

_____

_____

_____

Order of Events _____

_____

_____

_____

Transitional Words _____

Concluding Sentence(s) _____

_____

_____

On Your Own

Choose one of the topics from the Idea Box of think of one of your own. Complete this page. Then, write a narrative on another sheet of paper about how trash left in a park can be turned into something else.

Idea Box

○ Gloves and Mittens

○ Foam Food Containers

○ Newspapers

○ My Idea: _____

_____

_____

What Is Happening _____

_____

_____

Character _____

_____

Dialogue _____

_____

_____

_____

Order of Events _____

_____

_____

_____

Transitional Words _____

Concluding Sentence(s) _____

_____

_____

Name _____ Date _____

Student Assessment Checklist
Opinion Writing

1. Introduced the topic. .... ☐

2. Focused on the writing purpose. .... ☐

3. Addressed the audience appropriately. .... ☐

4. Stated an opinion. .... ☐

5. Developed and presented reasons, facts, and/or details
    to support an opinion. .... ☐

6. Organized the reasons, facts, and/or details in a logical order. ...... ☐

7. Connected the facts and opinion with linking words. .... ☐

8. Provided a concluding sentence. .... ☐

9. Wrote an opinion paragraph. .... ☐

More Things to Check

● Capitalized proper nouns. ☐

● Capitalized the first word of sentences. ☐

● Used correct punctuation. ☐

● Spelled words correctly. ☐

● Followed correct paragraph form. ☐

Writing Lessons to Meet the Common Core: Grade 5 © 2013 by Linda Ward Beech, Scholastic Teaching Resources

Name _____ Date _____

Student Assessment Checklist
Informative/Explanatory Writing

1. Introduced the topic. .... ☐

2. Focused on the writing purpose. .... ☐

3. Addressed the audience appropriately. .... ☐

4. Summarized or paraphrased information in notes. ..... ☐

5. Used facts and examples from research. .... ☐

6. Used definitions. .... ☐

7. Used details. .... ☐

8. Used subject-specific words and precise language. ..... ☐

9. Used linking words to connect ideas. .... ☐

10. Organized the information to help the reader. .... ☐

11. Listed steps. .... ☐

12. Included a quotation. .... ☐

13. Included an illustration. .... ☐

14. Provided a concluding sentence. .... ☐

15. Wrote an informative/explanatory paragraph. .... ☐

More Things to Check

● Capitalized proper nouns. ☐

● Capitalized the first word of sentences. ☐

● Used correct punctuation. ☐

● Spelled words correctly. ☐

● Followed correct paragraph form. ☐

Name _____ Date _____

Student Assessment Checklist
Narrative Writing

1. Focused on the writing purpose. .... ☐

2. Addressed the audience appropriately. .... ☐

3. Established the situation/setting. .... ☐

4. Established characters. .... ☐

5. Developed a good opening sentence. .... ☐

6. Organized the events in sequence. .... ☐

7. Used dialogue to show characters' responses. .... ☐

8. Used description. .... ☐

9. Used sensory words. .... ☐

10. Used transitional words. .... ☐

11. Provided a conclusion. .... ☐

12. Wrote a narrative. .... ☐

More Things to Check

● Capitalized proper nouns. ☐

● Capitalized the first word of sentences. ☐

● Used correct punctuation. ☐

● Spelled words correctly. ☐

● Followed correct paragraph form. ☐

Writing Lessons to Meet the Common Core: Grade 5 © 2013 by Linda Ward Beech, Scholastic Teaching Resources